AF375147

PASSION, PURPOSE, PROVISION

SHERRY BLACKMAN

Table of Contents

Introduction 1

Passion 3

Loneliness 9

Solitude 15

Wonder 23

Aging 27

Hospitality 33

Beauty 37

Exiles 43

Gratitude 47

Simplicity 51

Stone Babies 57

Winter 61

Travel 67

Creativity 73

Provision 77

Fields 83

Invest 91

Time 93

Regrets 95

Earth 99

Revolutionaries 101

Generosity 105

About the Author 111

Acknowledgments 113

Endnotes 115

To all daughters everywhere

Already

great

really

RECEIVED

Hello my dear

Dear Alice!

Thank you very much

Introduction

Dear Daughters,

I'm writing to you what I wished someone had written to me long ago as I wrestled with this magnificent thing called life. I long to share with you what decades of experience— of passion and indifference, of struggling to find purpose and then struggling to fulfill it, of provision and lack of it, of joy and sorrow—have written into me, onto my bones, if you will, a kind of spiritual hieroglyphics. I want to write about the mysteries of being human that weren't meant to be solved but lived into. I write these letters from a place of deep trembling.

Why write letters, something few bother with anymore? I want you to hold the same paper I hold, see my handwriting and signature as evidence that I existed. Let my letters be a kind of map and geography of who I am. In every word, see the jagged edges, cliffs, broken bones, wings, skies, stars, and oceans inside of me and how they might help you chart your own way through life.

You can tuck these testaments into a book, stuff them into your pocket, or leave them on a shelf. As you hold this book in your hands and flip the pages of these earnest letters, my hope is that you will feel held. I pray you will see the ink on these pages as scorch marks of the fire that burns in me, and yes, see the trees within the paper upon which I wrote.

May these "field notes" help strengthen your resolve and clarify a vision for your lives as you navigate through wild, uncharted places following your *calling*. What do I mean by *calling*? Again, I speak of mysteries—*calling* itself is a mystical word. There is a voice within us that sounds like our own but is under it, like a pulse, like a flame, beneath our skin. A voice still and small, heard when we are apart from all the noise, that calls out to us, telling us of the way to go. Trust it. Follow it.

There is so much I want to share with you in these letters before I leave this house of clay, before silence shrouds me and quiets my hands, not only of the mysteries of passion and purpose and provision but also of loneliness, solitude, simplicity, and so much more, that you might inhabit your own radiance.

Catch fire, my daughters.

Love,

S

Passion

Dear Daughters,

Find your sacred fire—your passion, that deep inner source of what gives you energy, love, and meaning—and you will answer the question of *why you are*.

Evolution doesn't answer what it *means* to be human, or why we desire passion and purpose and meaning for our lives, unlike creation stories. So let me begin with the creation story of Eden, a garden paradise, located between the Tigris and Euphrates Rivers in what would be Iraq today, according to ancient texts. Some believe Eden was a mythical place, yet the story of how a Creator breathed life into us explains why we are full of mysteries and longings. At our very beginning, passion was breathed into us, this fleshy composition of earth, wind, and fire.

There were two trees in Eden as the story goes, the Tree of Life and the Forbidden Tree of Knowledge of Good and Evil. Adam and Eve, the first humans, tended the garden and named all living things until the day they ate the forbidden fruit. For the first time, they knew shame and covered their nakedness with fig leaves, and they hid from the Creator who daily walked with them in the cool of the day.

They were banished then from paradise for their defiance. What fascinates me in this story is that when they ate the fruit, when they experienced sorrow and shame for the first time, they covered up the places of their fertility.

Whether Eden is a literal place or a myth, somehow, it's as if we hold a memory of this paradise, as if it is part of our DNA. We mourn our lost innocence, along with our peace, even as we continue to name everything living and nonliving, investigating the earth and stars and universes unknown. We carry our exile within us too. If we discover our passion, if we fan the flame of sacred fire that burns in us all, we will find a way back to paradise inside of us, to that garden where the Creator is, who I will name the *Presence* for the sake of these letters, who will be with us even as we journey through the hells of this life.

That fire is the sacred mystery of our being and humanity. It cannot be contained. It cannot hold one shape. It renews or destroys. Together, the Tree of Life and the Forbidden Tree burn there but are never consumed.

How are you to identify what your passion is? First, ask yourself: What enlivens you? What tears you open to everything? What drives your curiosity? What manna do you need to feast upon daily that increases your appetite for life itself? What makes you want to rise before the sun? What makes you feel as if you are born over and over again? In essence, what is written into every cell of your being?

Perhaps all these questions boil down to one simple query: What do you love to do above all else? And the most difficult, light-shedding question may be this: What makes you feel the most vulnerable?

Why vulnerability? Because fear is the fig leaf we hide

our creative being behind, the exile we carry within us, and the source of our "never good enough" shame.

What would you devote your life to if you knew you couldn't fail, no matter the suffering that may come with it?

This is your *why*. If you can answer these questions truthfully, you will know what you are meant to give your life to and to whom. Your *why* will be life-giving, transformative, and redemptive to others also.

Test your answers with these guiding principles: Will it bring beauty to the world? Will it reflect the light of the sacred fire, or will it be used for personal glory?

The mystery of passion is that while it sets your spirit aflame, the light of that fire offers a glimpse of paradise thought lost to those who look upon you. It will make you a lover of life and others without the worry of reciprocity.

So, start here. Sit quietly. Compose a life sentence, a mission statement, of how you want your life to read. Revise it as your days deepen, knowing provision will come if you maintain your focus. Read every word daily until it lands inside of you, until you've taken it in and come to believe it possible and achievable for yourself. Let these be stained glass words lit from the inside out, bearing witness of the greater, and the greatness in you.

I caution you. Few are true to themselves. Few are willing to give all that will be required, which is more than they think they have to give, until they give it. Living by fire will wring storms and sorrows out of you. It will ask you repeatedly what your name is. It will forbid the path of least resistance. It will test, torture, and consume you at times, for living close to the flame leaves a scar, especially when failure or rejection comes and provision is lacking.

I live the ecstasy and the agony of this truth and will share more of this in the letters that follow. I found ways to live out my two passions, writing and theology, and provision came in global adventures. I've interviewed world leaders, baptized infants in Kenya's rank slums, stood on the tarmac in Saudi Arabia as the first scud missiles were launched from Iraq, and so much more. Later in life, the doors swung open for me to enter seminary when I stopped listening to others tell me that I didn't belong in ministry because I was a woman.

Ask yourself how your passion might inform your work, your vocation, so you might make a living at what you love to do. Giving birth to oneself is never without its gestation and labor pains. We are enlarged in the waiting, in the creating, in what we will bring into the world.

High callings come with a high price. Are you willing to pay for it? Are you ready to stand and maintain your holy ground? Will you hold fast to the earth, wind, and fire that lives in your bone and marrow?

Most of us will not. It is too hard and there are too many obstacles, naysayers, and excuses to forsake the fire that never dies. Its embers remain even when we deny they exist or turn against ourselves in myriad ways.

Be intentional about living out your passion, which will define your purpose. Don't let others sentence you to a hollow-boned life you weren't meant to live. Accept complete ownership of your days, times, energies, and commitments.

There is no promise of easy provision. But there will be a willingness to live more simply and with less, for once you know who you are and whose you are, provision will come in many forms, sometimes even in seemingly impossible forms.

Be daughters of sacred fire. Live the mystery. Know that inside your passion is the *Presence* you long for.

Love,

S

Loneliness

Dear Daughters,

You say you suffer loneliness at times, and when you do, it is unbearable. It haunts and whispers of something or someone missing even when you are with others. Maybe the single most critical question loneliness asks is: *Who is missing?*

It might be the person you love who isn't present for whatever reason—someone lost, someone who has walked away. It might be a child your arms ache for who has grown up and flown the coop to build their own nest. It might be for a mother who is out of reach or a sister who has rejected you. It might be for mountains, forests, fields, or dunes.

Without a doubt, there are different types of loneliness, but each kind teaches us of our bond with all that lives. Loneliness is a sense of absence from our interconnectedness, a feeling of emptiness, as if the web we are all part of quivers and we are thrown off-balance, disrupted, detached from what holds us together.

Loneliness is a silent cry, a kind of sobbing, like when you fall and the wind is knocked out of you, and you gasp for air. When that happens, when that has happened to me,

I've discovered that it was me who was missing. Be reassured that everyone experiences feeling like they are outside the realm of the living at one time or another. Loneliness is an epidemic. I read a statistic recently that said forty-two percent of millennial women are more afraid of loneliness than a cancer diagnosis, according to one 2017 survey, and that was before the pandemic. Also, the survey reported that chronic loneliness could have the health effects of smoking fifteen cigarettes a day.[1]

In another 2019 survey conducted by health insurer Cigna, sixty-one percent of people feel lonely from "not enough social support, too few meaningful social interactions, poor physical and mental health, and not enough balance in our lives."[2]

To admit that one is lonely is to feel too vulnerable. It says something about our fears of being undesirable, unlovable, unwanted, of not being enough, that something is missing from us, in us, that it points to some failure or lack. Yet loneliness comes, a beggar at the door asking for food, and we might find our shelves are bare. We are hungry for skin and words and gazes, for human communion and completeness. We were created for such, but first, we must find the *Presence* in the absence.

This realization came home to me a few years ago on a hot July night when I sat across a bistro table from a fifty-one-year-old man, a hiker who had stayed at our church's hostel three years earlier. I didn't know him well, but I knew him in my bones. He was searching for more than forgiveness for his unfaithful, soon-to-be ex-wife. Even as we drank Australian wine from cheap, plastic cups, I saw that he was wrestling with an invisible angel who wanted to name him. He was like Jacob in the Hebrew bible who wrestled from night till dawn with an angel, unwilling to lose the battle. Then, as light broke, as the face of his opponent could barely be detected, the angel named him Israel and touched his thigh before departing so that he would walk with a limp for the rest of his life and never forget the mysterious being he'd prevailed against.

Two things I take away from this story, among many other life-giving lessons: We suffer injuries in this life, we walk with our limps, but we are renamed if we prevail so that we might live beyond our singularity, so that we might make room for others, for community, for what and who is yet to come. Israel became the name of a nation.

Loneliness pushes us to find the holy in the human within ourselves first, so that we are not looking for another human being to complete us—not a spouse, partner, child, or friend. It is too great of a burden to place upon another person to fulfill all our longings. The beggar named Loneliness reminds us of the deeper hunger raging within us, never satisfied until we find the *Presence*, the One, who some call God, a name I don't want to use in these letters because it has lost its meaning, identity, and power in this age.

Human love is never enough, as essential as it is. It is but a door through which we must all pass to find home. Poet Rainer Maria Rilke says God is "the great homesickness we could never shake off."[3]

That homesickness is what I tried to share with my friend that summer night. He once had faith but had lost it along the way, and as we spoke about how lonely he was, I said something that surprised me. "I am five years into learning to be alone, but the gift of loneliness has been to fully own myself and my life, my passions, my mistakes, my past—all of me, the good, the bad, the ugly. It's not been easy. It's a lot to deal with. So I didn't want to dive into another relationship to avoid the pain of it all. For me, I had to find what lay beneath my loneliness, or what was inside of it, who or what was missing."

Listening to myself, I understood I'd wrested those words from days and years of rising in the morning without someone to cook breakfast or dinner for—not a son, daughter, or husband—after nearly four decades of shaping and structuring my life around family. Words wrested from betrayals and traumas and abandonments rose within me as if each syllable sounded and spoken was a scribble of veins and arteries.

It took me years and two divorces to discover what that gift is and the power of it, to take complete responsibility and possess my life. I committed to learning whatever lesson I was unwilling to learn earlier in my life after my second divorce had left me profoundly wounded. I remember this terrible ache, a throbbing inside when my divorce was finalized days before Christmas 2012. I attended a party with some colleagues from the college where I was teaching. There was a professor there that I had known for fifteen years, a gentle man, a poet, and all I wanted was to lay next to him on his bed that was piled high with coats. I wanted nothing more than for him to hold me. I never gave voice to that ache, didn't act on that impulse. I knew sorrow has its own speech, and it echoed in all my silences. I knew better. I understood it was my vulnerability, defeat, and loss that imagined his arms would keep my fractured soul from shattering all over the place.

During chaplaincy training, my supervisor told me I suffered from organizational avoidance, meaning that I organized my life in ways to avoid confronting whatever it was I was running away from. I have thought long and hard about that. He was right about how I had always gotten lost in my work, though only to find, honestly, my truest self. For me, that was not getting lost. After my first failed marriage, I dated shortly after and was convinced I had grieved enough while I was in the marriage. I discovered there's a different kind of mourning once a marriage is over and you aren't living together anymore. I hadn't fully mourned the lost dream, the loss of innocence, the perceived and real damage to my children.

After my second divorce nearly twenty years later, I grieved both marriages. I committed myself to endure my darkest nights at a time when everything else was falling apart around me—a child whose partner and father of her children almost killed her one night, another child in the throes of active addiction that was carving her body and mind up into swallowable pieces.

Lament will find its way into us no matter how hard we work to keep it at bay. It is an ocean, a sea, with its tides and weather and storms. A sea without boundaries.

I turned inward. I endured the darkness. When I could not deal with the anxiety of loneliness, sometimes the sheer terror of it, I would go kayaking or hiking, something that forced me to focus on the physicality of life, on my breath, as if the *Presence* was recreating me, breathing wholeness into my brokenness.

We were created for love, companionship, and intimacy. In the beginning, the story goes that Adam gave up a rib, let his bones be broken so as not to be alone, even though he had the Creator to walk with in the cool of the day. The holy and the human—we need both. We were made for love and will never be satisfied without it. Human love awakens us to holy love, and holy love stirs us to love even when it is not returned. Without loneliness, we would never discover that we are never alone, even as we long for human company, for touch, for the strength of an arm around us.

When you suffer loneliness, go outside and stare at the sky, watch the trees move from an unseen force, feel the sun on your face, the warmth, and know that the *Presence* is gazing at you in the light of the sun, stars, and moon. When you are struck as if by some inner lightning that splits you apart, muster the courage enough to stay in the storm, to sit in the dark that shutters the stars. Wait until dawn when the birds sing their heart out into the wild, telling each other their name. I am convinced that we all must find the One in the darkness before we can live fully in the light.

C. S. Lewis wrote, "We are born helpless. As soon as we are fully conscious, we discover loneliness. We need others physically, emotionally, and intellectually. We need them if we are to know anything, even ourselves."[4]

That night, sitting across the table from the hiker, I said I had finally discovered what theologian Meister Eckart, who'd lived over eight hundred years ago, had meant when he wrote, "There's a place in the soul where you've never been wounded." That is the inner sanctum that loneliness will lead us to if we seek what is true, where we come wounded, listening for our name—the Holy of Holies where *Presence* exists in every human being.

Love,

S

Solitude

Dear Daughters,

Solitude, like mystery and beauty, is one of our deepest needs. Yes, needs. Most of us haven't the skills nor the courage to know what to do with the spiritual fevers that inflame us.

Years ago, I asked a forty-eight-year-old woman how she would feel if she had to stay home all day by herself. She was a kinetic person, always running to and from something, maybe grief, maybe shame, or maybe some other unnamed fear. She lived in a nice house in a swanky lake community with her husband, two daughters, and a dog. I'll never forget her answer.

She said, "I'd be terrified."

It wasn't loneliness that scared her, but the simple, profound act of being alone with herself, apart from the world, a different kind of trembling than loneliness. So why is being alone so terrifying?

Because that is where the wound is, where our longings and laments cry out, and where our healing waits. Here we come face-to-face with our moral injuries—the things we've done, the things done to us—that hold us hostage.

Terror comes, but on its heels the dark hands of solitude soothe us with a kind of holy salve.

A chaplain serving at an in-patient rehab for those battling addiction tells his clients, "Unless you go to that hard place, your lives won't be different. They won't change. It's scary and hurtful. You must feel that anger, sadness, and reckon all your emotions, not medicate or suppress them—that's the part everyone wants to skip. You must sit with the uncomfortableness of it, the terror of it."

In 2014, *Science Journal* reported that people detest being made to spend six to fifteen minutes in a room by themselves with nothing to do but think—even to the extent of being willing to give themselves mild electric shocks instead.[5]

This is no new phenomenon. Blaise Pascal, a fifteenth-century French philosopher, wrote, "All of humanity's problems stem from man's inability to sit quietly in a room alone." And that was long before there was enough technology to guarantee we could live in a state of constant distraction.

Alone, venturing into the mystery of solitude, courage will come to us and name the wounds that infect our lives. I suffered the wound of abandonment inflicted upon me when I was young. My father slowly, painfully, silently, left the family, no longer husband to my mother, no longer "Dad" to his four children. Around that same time, when I was fifteen, I was date-raped by a boy I cared for and who I thought cared for me. There was no word for "date rape" back then. It was always the girl's fault for being in a situation where the violation could occur. It was her shame and stupidity. Such betrayals and desertions led me to abandon and disown myself.

Solitude became my enemy then, shame a faithful companion. I hated, feared, being all alone.

I left high school after my junior year to attend college and then matriculated to a hospital-based three-year nursing program. I decided on this noble profession against a career in fashion design, which others said was highly competitive and not a sound choice. I translated that to mean I didn't have what it takes to succeed. I loved to write, but my parents discouraged me from such a precarious profession. It didn't take me long to discover I couldn't bear the suffering of others, and I swooned while plunging a needle into an orange for practice while in my second year of nursing school. But it was during this struggle at nursing school, feeling disappointed with myself once again, away from the chaos and emotional wreckage back home, when I had to accept who I was, who I am, who I will always be. I could only heal, I knew, if I refused to abandon myself.

I took a leave of absence mid-second year, returned home to tell my parents over Christmas that I had left nursing school, and told my father I wanted to transfer to a college where the poet, the writer in me, could develop. My father said I would never put bread on the table as a writer and refused to send me. Provision always came first for my parents' generation, and I am grateful for all they provided. That was their highest priority. They had experienced World War II, had grown up during the Great Depression, and they knew hunger. It was with the best intentions that they wanted me to place provision first in my life choices as well. I tried to tell my dad writing was my bread. Was I naive? Yes. Yet this love was something so powerful in me that I refused to deny or abandon myself no matter what. My open wounds became wells of passion.

My father abandoned me differently then, but no less devastatingly. He had always believed in my intelligence. I had been an honor student throughout high school, college, and nursing school. But he didn't understand how rooted the passion, the drive, was in me to write, nor how strong-willed I could be. I entered the most spiritual place on earth when creating. I was held by mystery, plunged into liminal space, freshly born. Everything within me sang of everything that is. I was visible, yet wonderfully invisible. I dissolved into song, became part of something so much greater than myself. I was but one note in this mighty opus called life.

Yet, I was tenuous, afraid to be utterly alone, untethered all on my own, with no emotional or financial support, career-less, school-less, partner-less for the first time in my life. I was found at the same time that I was lost. How could I be a writer without further education? I wasn't good enough.

I was vulnerable to my aching insecurities, feeling disowned again even as I began to own myself. I met a man soon after leaving school and returning home who had also dropped out of college. We married eight months later. It didn't take me long to understand one of life's greatest lessons—no other human being, no partner, no spouse, no "other" is responsible for my happiness, completeness, or fulfillment. We both worked hard. I cleaned houses, was a mother's helper, then managed a small retail store. I had just turned twenty before we married. A little over a year later, I was pregnant. My dream of being a writer haunted my waking and sleeping but remained a dream.

Motherhood was, in some sense, an exodus into a different wilderness. My firstborn grew in the cradle of my bones, in the secret place of my being. She made it hard to breathe sometimes, a foot under a rib, her spine pressing into mine. She kicked me from the inside out as nothing other than another human being could do. I would be *two*, never *one* again, as time uttered days for the rest of my life.

Born, she was a six-pound civilization of dreams and storms and wonder. A solid breath of God held in my quivering hands. My daughter's presence forced me to acknowledge further the unnamed wounds and the wild things that roamed and taunted and lived in them. Her cries shattered me like howls in the night. I feared I would ruin her even though I loved her more than I had ever loved anyone. Love flowed from me like the rivers of milk that rushed from my body to nourish and keep her alive.

Holding her, I held myself. We were both unspoken. Her name was my name. It was then, exhausted, slippery with July heat, battling through postpartum depression, that I stopped being afraid of being alone. I longed for the womb of solitude, a place of gestation, for in it was my fertility, and like pregnancy itself, it happens in darkness.

And it cost me.

My young husband was afraid of who *I Am*. To embrace me and the holy fire within me meant he would lose me, he thought, when in truth it would have drawn me closer to him.

When we moved into our second home, now a family of four and married for twelve years, there was a spare bedroom I wanted as my writing studio. But my husband wouldn't "let" me have it for myself. Instead, he insisted on sharing it as office space. By then, I had begun to publish in newspapers and magazines, was back in college, and dared to call myself a writer. However, I still felt like a fraud when I said it since the novels and books in my drawer went unpublished, rejected, despite the praise and encouragement from agents and publishers.

This desire for a room of my own was a battle I refused to lose. It was but one expression of this war in my marriage for space, for a sense of worth and identity and separateness. When we sought marriage counseling, my husband told the counselor, "Her writing is the only thing I can't control in her."

Decades later, long after our divorce, I think that I failed to love the wounds in him. The ones he couldn't or wouldn't expose or let them weep themselves clean. He could not, like me for so long, press the tender, swollen places of his pain.

I wonder how many women, daughters all, have forfeited their lives to someone who insisted on controlling them out of fear of losing them? How many fear their own lives so much that they become prisoners to security and status quo and forfeit themselves out of the sheer fear of failure and being alone? How many hide behind their children or partners or careers because they were afraid to be who they were created to be? How many never endure the labor of birthing oneself, listening instead to the names everyone else gives them or insists on calling them?

I've learned that no one will fight for you if you do not stand up for yourself. The wilderness is our training ground.

We learn courage only by wandering the unmapped places, knowing sometimes you have to be lost before you can be found. Such is the training ground for warriors who will stand up and fight for their daughters.

Solitude is a wilderness that tests and reveals us to ourselves, awakens our senses, ripens our spirituality, sets our souls on fire, purifies, and cauterizes our wounds. This exodus into the unknown place, into silence and aloneness, is essential for knowing who we are. If we refuse the journey, we court the worst kind of disaster. If we abandon ourselves, we abandon everyone else in a crucial way.

It has taken me a lifetime to understand what author Marianne Williamson meant when she wrote:

> Our deepest fear is not that we are inadequate. Our deepest fear is that we are powerful beyond measure. It is our light, not our darkness that most frightens us. We ask ourselves, Who am I to be brilliant, gorgeous, talented, fabulous? Actually, who are you not to be? You are a child of God. Your playing small does not serve the world. There is nothing enlightened about shrinking so that other people won't feel insecure around you. We are all meant to shine, as children do. We were born to make manifest the glory of God that is within us. It's not just in some of us; it's in everyone. And as we let our own light shine, we unconsciously give other people permission to do the same. As we are liberated from our own fear, our presence automatically liberates others.[6]

Without traversing this wilderness, we will not find our greatest fertility and grow our lives. Solitude is required for creativity. It allows us to journey into the vast universe that exists within us, where no one else can see, even as it rubs up against our skin. So don't be afraid to stare into your wounds until they become live-giving sources.

Daughters, be pregnant with yourselves always.

Be fertile. Find the *I Am* in you.

Love,

S

Wonder

Dear Daughters,

Solitude and wonder are partner mysteries. One invites us into stillness, the other to investigate, interrogate, parse, and remember. Both widen the aperture of our vision and expand the possibilities of our lives.

Wonder is the prelude to creativity, passion, purpose, and provision. It winnows out what doesn't belong. It lives the open-ended questions, ever conscious of the mysteries. Such gives oxygen to the sacred fire that burns brightest when we engage and cross-examine what we see and don't see, understand and don't understand, feel and don't feel. Boundless love lives inside awe, which is why we feel so alive when we wonder.

So, walk around stunned, open-mouthed, and curious. Fear no question, ask them all, and challenge the imagination. Wrestle with "what ifs." Without this kind of reverence pulsing in our blood, we will not hear what's been spoken into the stars, rivers, and seas. Awe enlivens us to rapture, to see and dream and remember. It wakes our thirst for, and a stirring of, the deepest waters of our existence.

The *Presence* swims with us in our mothers' wombs. There, the knowing begins and eternity whispers to us.

Once born, the memory of the *Presence* diminishes as the scent of the inward sea fades from our skin. We forget what we've always known. Yet, there's a map inside us to the way home, buried under the shale-like years of our lives.

Go back to what you know. Rise early in the morning and spend long moments staring out windows or sitting outdoors. Gaze at sunrises, at the sky's grayness and brightness. Lose yourselves to the quietness and to the dreams you had the night before. Sip coffee and feel the air's currents tousle your hair. Question how every voice has a distinct sound, is identifiable, owned, unshared, a musical composition, proof of individuality. Consider how a song rises out of your throat like angels parting a sea. Soak up everything into the vast universe beneath your skin. Nurture your imagination. Without imagination, there would be no recall, no memories, no concept of the unseen, no faith, no hope. Remember everything. Pay attention to the details and intricacies. Memorize the hands of someone you love or have loved.

I recall my father's hands on the last day of his life—the paled freckles, the swollen blue veins, the weakened and erratic pulse at his wrist, and the ridged, square fingernails like rows of small gardens waiting for seed. His fingers weakly interlaced mine, and I could sense all the days he had held me, lugging me to and fro and carrying my sleepy body to bed when I was young, and holding me when I wept as a grown woman. He's pressed into me forever. On this last day, his fingertips turned purple. Death started at the far ends of him and inched its way up.

Look intently at everything around you. In the novel *Long Way Gone*, Charles Martin writes that his guitar is more than it is—it's a mistress, a sabbath, a rock, a flying carpet, where light invades the dark and rolls the darkness back.[7]

I end this letter with some more quotes that will, I hope, heat your blood and give you the courage to live the hardest questions, to contemplate the humming mystery of our being-ness, and to uncover the map hidden within.

Carl Sagan, an American astronomer and planetary scientist, wrote in his book *Cosmos*, "The Cosmos is all that is or was or ever will be. Our feeblest contemplations of the Cosmos stir us—there is a tingling in the spine, a catch in the voice, a faint sensation, as if a distant memory of falling from a height. We know we are approaching the greatest of mysteries."[8]

To quote Einstein, "Imagination is more important than knowledge…imagination embraces the entire world, and all there ever will be to know and understand." Also, "What I see in Nature is a magnificent structure that we can comprehend only very imperfectly, and that must fill a thinking person with a feeling of humility."

And this one by Saint Augustine: "Men go abroad to wonder at the heights of mountains, at the huge waves of the sea, at the long courses of the rivers, at the vast compass of the ocean, at the circular motions of the stars, and they pass by themselves without wondering."

Wonder, daughters, about all that is, and dream and

imagine and investigate. The mysteries will never be exhausted, and with each interrogation, your lives will expand in all directions.

Love,

S

Aging

Dear Daughters,

I've watched my mother grow old. It is strange to say the words *grow* and *old* together as if speaking with two tongues. Yet, I've witnessed the hidden grace of thinning days, the humility of time, even as the physical body fades and weakens and laments toward silence.

My mother is about to turn ninety-eight. Everyone comments on her beauty. Random people stop her on sidewalks as she walks haltingly to tell her she's gorgeous. She's worn her dyed blonde hair in a Marilyn Monroe style for the last seven or more decades, which makes me chuckle. Somehow, she still manages to pull it off. Apple-red lipstick is her shade of choice, applied on her lips, tightened into a small circle.

During World War II, she trained with the Army Corps of Nurses at Syracuse University and worked as a registered nurse until she was eighty-nine, caring for the elderly who were sometimes decades younger than her. When my father grew increasingly absent in her late forties, every minister and lawyer advised her to seduce him back home with kindness and love, to bleed alone, to bite her tongue until severed, to protect him. She taught me about ways women kill themselves long before dying. Within a few years, she developed breast cancer as if trauma and abandonment were the architects of this disease that ravaged the nurturing place in her. She had a radical mastectomy. After surgery, in her anesthetic stupor, she whispered to my father that he could stay with the kids since she wouldn't be home.

I recently learned that my grandfather, my father's father, had told her he thought that maybe my father left her for someone else because she'd had a hysterectomy a few years earlier due to a medical condition. Need I say how angry I became when she told me that? I asked her how she responded.

"With silence," she said.

Swallow your tongue for no one.

In time, as she fought a war of independence she never willingly enlisted in, she won herself. She prayed for a husband for many years, until one day she heard God say to her that He wanted her all for himself. To this day, I will always be grateful she listened to that voice. Our home became a refuge for spiritual seekers. No one was ever turned away from our table. No conversation was taboo. She traveled to faraway places, including the Holy Land, adventures I doubt she would have had if she had been married to my father.

It's her humor and ability to laugh at herself that has been as much of a gift as her strength, faith, and love for others. She's always struggled with unfamiliar names. For example, her brother served as a missionary in Niger and had adopted an orphaned African girl named Marianna. Marianna grew up to be a doctor and came to the United

States often to visit her American family who had retired in Indiana decades earlier. Recently, my mother learned that Marianna had died. When my mother spoke to my brother, she said, "I was so sorry to hear about marijuana." She almost died, literally, laughing at her slip of the tongue. She couldn't catch her breath.

Whenever we are together, she tells the stories of her life, of the apple orchard on the small farm in upstate New York where she grew up. She returns, it seems, to innocence she's never lost. She'd cart her dolls under their arches, lay down a blanket, and have a tea party among the trees she named Emily, Elizabeth, Jane, Mary….

She knew their white blossom rain, sweet fruit, bruised windfalls. She pruned their branches alongside her father so that these women could bear a greater harvest. Her father taught her also how to graft one tree into another.

Now her bones and hands are like the branches she once cut away, gnarled, knobby, and brittle. Her spine bends toward the earth as if remembering her roots. Things have fallen from her life, been plucked too. Still, she has borne a great harvest beyond her children and grandchildren and great-grandchildren. She's planted seeds of wisdom, kindness, and compassion in gardens unknown.

She's lived all the seasons of the apple tree now.

Soon, she'll be grafted into eternity, even though just writing those words makes me weep. I picture her lying down inside an endless orchard, abundant with all kinds of fruit, with radiant petals raining down upon her, her arms extended in praise.

Where is the grace in *growing* old? I've seen the light that once shone on her face dim and go inward. She cannot form a fist, her hands cannot grasp things—she holds the world more loosely now. Neither can she hear as well as she once could—not the songs of birds, or children laughing, or the voices of her sons and daughters. She cannot see as sharply anymore. A pulse pounds weaker at her wrist under her papery skin scribbled with blue veins.

But what if the losses she's experienced really are a ripening? What if we lose the outer world so that we will pay closer attention to "the deep innerness of all things," as the Poet Rainer Maria Rilke would say?

What's lived and unlived in us, loved and unloved, known and unknown, is written into every cell of our bodies. Yet, as the losses that come with age darken our days, the light within glows brighter. This is the lamp by which we read our lives and speak it out.

This may be the only way we can willingly liberate and let go of this glorious, beautiful life. Even in all its losses and suffering, it is too magnificent to want to leave life behind. This existence is all we know. We pack up our senses, strength, courage, and will for a destination unknown, even as we've carried a memory and a deep homesickness for Eden all our days.

My mother's passage into old age has forced me to deal with a reality that most of us try to convince ourselves will never happen. How do you go with life rather than fight it? How do you not fear the invisibility that comes with aging in our culture, unlike other cultures where the elderly are revered?

Her mother, my grandmother, used to say that unless she looks in the mirror, she thinks of herself as sixteen. She died at ninety-nine. One's spirit grows and matures, but is it not ageless? Is not eternity written into us? Is that why we say we *grow* old?

As we age, the invisible comes into sharper focus. I remember hearing about a grandfather who was fishing off a dock with his young grandson. The grandson asked, "Grandpa, how can you believe in God when you can't see him?" The grandfather replied, "Son, God is about *all* I see now."

Maybe the key to growing old gracefully is to let go of all else but grace. Let its white blossoms rain upon us and its orchard cradle us. Let the arms and hands of the apple trees hold us as wind swirls its fragrance and seeds upon us, whispering of the beauty, mystery, and wonder of all that is and of what is yet to come.

Love,

S

Already

great

really

Hello my dear

RECEIVED

Dear Alice!

Thank you very much

Hospitality

Dear Daughters,

I have a table made of mesquite wood that is eight feet long and thirty inches wide. Before it was a table, it was a door to a mission in the Southwest. It is grooved, seamed, and gapped with raised half-inch round nail heads that make for a perfectly uneven surface. Prior to topping it with plexiglass, you had to pay close attention to where you placed your cup or glass, or it would easily tip over. A metal lock centers one side, and on the other, notches mark where the hinges were. It has the weight of the forest in it and requires two strong people to lift or move it.

Sitting around it is to consider its home, the tree it once was, upon which birds landed, nested, and sang. A tree that knew wind and rain, maybe snow, sunlight, maybe a child's hands and arms. A tree grounded in soil that was home to a million different life forms whose roots reached out to anchor other trees underground, holding them steady during storms the same ways hands reach out across the table to pass food, to comfort, and pray. A living thing, cut down, sawed, planed, glued, gouged, nailed, and screwed together—transformed from one life form to another.

A door now serving as a table is a perfect metaphor for what a table represents, symbolizing the entrance into lives, into *communis,* where family, friends, and strangers gather, where meaning, belonging, and accountability is cultivated.

The table is, in its own way, a room. By far the most important *room* in a home. Here we "break bread" in the same way we break ourselves open to each other while looking one another in the eye. We say a word of gratitude together before sharing a meal. We embody grace by being there side by side and across from one another. Every person gathered around it, a thousand reasons to love.

The table is a celebration of provision, nourishing body, mind, and spirit. So I share some simple advice: keep it free of papers and piles. Instead, place something beautiful at its center so that it remains an open, wordless invitation to any who enter your dwelling.

When I think back on the tables I have sat around, my mother's holds the weight of generations—her mother, children, grandchildren, and great-grandchildren—and lifelong friends who gathered around it every week for decades to pray for each other. She and my father purchased it shortly after they were married in 1946, right after World War II ended, after my father's discharge from the army.

Now, seventy-five years later, the black walnut table has loose joints and needs refinishing. The veneer and varnish are worn or flaked off in several places. There are two leaves to extend the length of the table, but one of them came from somewhere else. It doesn't belong, but my mother, now ninety-eight years old, insists on keeping it even though it slips and slides out of place, creating a balancing act for anyone seated at that intersection. The table seems to have held onto every word spoken across its grain, absorbed the bouts of breathless laughter, soaked in all the prayers spoken and unspoken across it, as well as all the eye-rolling, glances, tears, and a few battles.

As a young child, I remember staring at the peas I had slipped into my glass of milk when I thought no one was looking. When I was older, my brother pitched a glass of milk on my sister when she was harassing him about his girlfriend. Birthday parties, anniversary celebrations, Sunday dinners, spur-of-the-moment afternoon tea—all here. Many of my friends came to my mother's table a long time ago and found a refuge to discuss whatever was on their minds or breaking their hearts. No matter who showed up last minute, there was always enough food to go around—my mother turned no one away. She taught me that hospitality is far more than a welcoming home, open arms, or a gourmet meal. It's about lingering long after dessert is served and finished because once you start to clear the dishes, the conversation ends.

The table is a door we open, a room we invite others into to strengthen the invisible, intimate web that holds all things together. As you grow in your passion and focus on your purpose, let the table be a symbol of provision. What you give returns to you, so give of your time, place, and energy, and the world of possibility will open to you. Make "room" for others.

Love,

S

Beauty

Dear Daughters,

Russian novelist Fyodor Dostoevsky wrote, "The awful thing is that beauty is mysterious as well as terrible. God and the devil are fighting there and the battlefield is the heart of man."[9]

Dostoevsky was right. Beauty is mysterious as well as terrible. We want to swallow it whole, contain it. We worship and crave and covet its power, yet it's elusive. Spiritual in nature, beauty is an ache, a longing, a hunger, a gravitational pull toward what is beyond us, within us, outside of us. It lacerates and pierces, keeps us from falling off the edges of the world, instills hope, teaches us there is more to what we cannot see than what we do see.

Perhaps most beautiful are our scars, the evidence of our injuries and healings, reminders of life's fragility. What's left behind in the dark, pink, white, rope-like, or hollow marks, in the damage and disfigurement, is proof of life lived and endured, proof that we stumbled and raised up, that we risked and overcame.

Beauty hides in groundless places like sorrow when we are most awake and vulnerable. Perhaps it's most mysterious in the old, when it is distilled and empties itself fully into us, hiding in the shadows of an aging face and in the eyes that see through this canvas of skin to the artist within.

This subject is far too complex to dissect in a simple letter, but it's imperative that I address this topic because beauty is terrible when it misleads, stalls, abuses, or impales the human spirit. Women are driven to be beautiful, steered by a culture that insists on objectifying the female body. Women have adorned themselves since the beginning of time, and every generation has its particular notion of attractiveness—tight hair, loose, messy, or lacquered; red lipstick, false eyelashes, thick brows, blue eyeshadow, iridescent bronzes. The lucrative cosmetic industry preys on our insecurities, magnifies our imperfections, and breeds discontentment—*it knows we mistake admiration for love* and offers us a skin-deep version of our deepest desires.

There is a kind of spiritual bankruptcy when women obsess about their physical appearance at the neglect of their God-given passion and purpose. Health and self-care are essential. Both will reflect or deflect the magnificence in each of us.

Don't degrade yourselves by wearing pajamas in public, walking around unkempt, or dressing too provocatively. People make snap judgments based on appearance even though we deny it—it happens almost unconsciously. We tell people how we think of ourselves by how we present ourselves, no matter where we are. One question that is worth asking ourselves is, on what do we want the other's attention to focus upon?

Obsessing over one's appearance is common among

young girls trying to make the world aware of them, but some never grow out of that form of enslavement. If a woman's only perceived power is her ability to attract or seduce, she will fade away, deflate as the years go on, while scrambling to keep her physical appearance youthful at all costs, literally. When older women go through all kinds of machinations to pretend they are not as old as they are, they become unrecognizable versions of themselves.

Years ago, after interviewing a dermatologist for an article on aging, she offered me free Botox injections that paralyze the muscles in the face so that wrinkles become less visible. When I told my family physician, he was angry, said such an injection erases one's facial expressions so that they can no longer be read, interpreted, or understood. It's like having Amyotrophic Lateral Sclerosis (also known as ALS or Gehrig's disease). I didn't go.

What ultimately makes us most beautiful isn't complicated. Are we communicating love, care, acceptance, and the desire to be in the company of the other? Do we laugh? I doubt there is anything more bonding than laughing together. Anne Lamott says, "Laughter is a bubbly, effervescent form of holiness."

If, as the good book says, our bodies are temples, then they are inhabited by the sacred. We encounter *Presence* in this cathedral of flesh and bone. Others experience *Presence* in us if we choose what is soul-deep, not skin-deep alone. So let beauty seduce us to choose authenticity and self-sacrifice over the superficial and the artificial. Let beauty empty us, then fill us, the way music does, before it rushes back to the battlefield.

Love,

S

P.S. I wrote this untitled poem long ago. It fell out
of a book I randomly picked up as I was writing
this letter, so I thought I'd share it.

An old man I did not know
wheeled himself to my side.
He spoke of beauty
out of his withering.

He said, "Progress destroys beauty."
Age had whitened and spotted his skin dark.
His teeth, gray and mossy.
His words crooked but decipherable.
Across the street, men—
paid to have no conviction,
chopped at an ancient tree.
Axe dissecting rings of time—

I heard seeds scream—
bark rip and fall—
arms shatter, roots sob—
a soul throb.

I looked at the old man,
wondered at the cries in his hands
and eyes that sounded like my own.
I wanted to ask him about the glory of his youth—

We stared at the broken tree.
How close it had grown to Heaven,
to the core of winds, to the voice of sky
and the aria of stars.

Its branches held me day after day
even though I remained on the ground,
like a father holds his son,
like a mother her daughter

even when they are distances apart.
I wanted to cradle that old man,
crippled, limbs twisted inward,
as beautiful to me as that tree once stood.

I looked again to the world—
at men chipping the wooden body
until there was no evidence of its life.
I longed for it—

yearned to carry a bone of it away—
just to breathe and remember
what is forever lost and never preserved—
ancient trees and old, beautiful men.

Exiles

Dear Daughters,

A fifty-year-old professional man wept as he confessed his multiple extra-marital affairs and alcoholism. "It cost me too much," he said. "I don't want to live a dishonest life anymore."

One late Sunday afternoon, another man about the same age belted back a few shots and nursed a beer at a local pub, saying he frequented the watering hole as he did not want to go home to an empty house. He was lonely. His ten-year affair had caught up with him, ending his thirty-year marriage.

A woman in her forties, in recovery from addiction, shared how looking back on her life, she wondered what she'd missed. The unknown haunted her with "what could have been."

Both darkness and light chase us. We surrender to one or the other. And yet, the mystery is that the light exposes the darkness and teaches us what is true and false, what gives life and what steals it. Without both, we would never know who we are, what we are capable of, or how long and far we cast our shadow.

Again, we go back to the story of our beginning, no matter how we chose to understand it, whether as mythology or metaphor, as true or not. Two trees flourished in the Garden of Creation—the Tree of Life and the Tree of the Knowledge of Good and Evil. One ensured life, the other promised death. In Islam, the Tree of the Knowledge of Good and Evil is also called the Tree of Pain. Once Adam and Eve ate from the Tree of Pain, they knew torment and were exiled from paradise.

It's a wonder—what was it about that tree that lured Adam and Eve to pluck its fruit? Were its flowers so fragrant, its petals so silken, its stamens so alluring that it didn't take much for the tempter to convince them to partake of it? And, when they sank their teeth into its succulent flesh and the juices ran down their necks, was the taste of death at first sweet, like the taste of darkness too often can be?

The fruit of the Tree of Life and the Tree of Pain is forever in our mouths and bloodstream. We swallow night and day in the same bite. We speak in fragments now the name of everything, our words both sweet and bitter. Our language, broken. We remember innocence and perfection. It's embedded in our ancestral memory, and our exile tortures us.

The seeds, the embryos of the fruit of both trees, are planted deep within us. The question is, which one will we cultivate in our lives? If we cultivate the Tree of Pain's poisonous seeds, we will be blind to what is beautiful and good and glorious. They will suffocate the sacred fire within until we don't want to live at all or until we've had enough of death. If we choose the Tree of Life, we will know aliveness and the vibrancy that belongs to each of us, so live carefully.

Indulge me for a moment to speak of three deadly seeds from the Tree of Pain that I have seen destroy too many lives and the lives of those around them. One is the seed of substance abuse—it has an energy of its own. It will grow up like a mighty tree that will cut off the light for all growth below. Its vines will choke to death one's passion, strength, ambition, self-possession, dignity, integrity, and relationships. When we hear people say, "I'm wasted," they're telling the truth. Children are sacrificed on the altar of addiction, marriages ruined, bodies ravaged, society compromised, and our economy undermined.

Two is the seed of excessive entertainment that ushers in complacency and apathy, distracting and pacifying us, devouring essential time, solitude, and silence. Life requires that we show up for it and live it. It requires intention, work, and protection. Focus is lost when we indulge in this way. It's crucial that we write our life sentence, our mission statement so we don't forget why we are here. Without a vision for our lives, a map, we will have no direction.

Three, the seed of consumerism. William Wordsworth wrote, "The world is too much with us; late and soon. Getting and spending, we lay waste our powers."[10] Refuse to lay waste your powers to debt, bankruptcy, and greed—the more generous your investment in others, the greater the return. Material things never satisfy for long; the adrenaline rush of buying fades rather quickly when the bills come in.

Know this, that when people say, "I hit bottom," it's a moment of reckoning. The fact that there is a bottom and not an endless fall is proof of the grace that lives in the center of our being. We all need to get back to our center where the Tree of Life grows, where we can sow what gives life—love, mercy, compassion, kindness, accountability, and generosity. Remember what we do to ourselves, we do to others. What we do to others, we do to ourselves.

Exile or return, death or life, is hidden and uttered in everything we cultivate. We are residents of Eden even while we are exiles. Paradise is within us, even as the taste of forbidden fruit is forever on our tongues. We salivate to know what we should never know. And when we eat of the Tree of Pain, we suffer and cause suffering. It swallows us up. We lose our innocence again and again. We believe our exile is forever, that the Tree of Life is unreachable, that we have strayed too far, that forgiveness is impossible. But the Tree of Life is right there, inside us forever, and its roots can strangle the mighty Tree of Pain until it withers. Light will always wring out the darkness.

Love,

S

Gratitude

Dear Daughters,

Not long ago, I received a text from a loved one thanking me for something I had done. I immediately felt stones drop from my voice, freeing it from held-on-to hurts that graveled my throat. For a long time, I'd felt unappreciated, invisible, taken for granted, unloved really, until a few words, texted no less, made me feel as if I could walk on water.

Giving and receiving gratitude makes for fertile lives. Things burst out of us. There is a grand release of love, a physical heightening of the senses. Limbs lighten, lungs enlarge, hands bloom. Our blindness subsides, our veins open for a transfusion of light and oxygenates our blood.

The bittersweet truth is that life and death lie in the power of the tongue. We live in words, and words live in us. They pulse, brighten, rouse, unite, or shatter, scatter, assassinate, and fragment. Silence kills, too, when it's weaponized. Much is heard in the sign language of gesture and expression, in the turning away or the turning toward another. The body has a built-in lie detector—it tells the truth even when our mouths do not.

So be intentional with your speech. Speak out what

encourages and builds up even if you are the only person in the room. You will never run out of things to be grateful for, ever. All you need to do is look and see and listen. Everything is already here to feel the great force of gratitude that wakes us to beauty and mystery, for what is sacred and eternal. Awakened, generosity and tenderness flow out of us, strengthens our bones, heals our relationships and un-numbs us, all the while repairing the frayed strands of the divine-human web.

Refuse to muzzle your praise. In everything, nothing excluded, give thanks. Yes, it's an act of faith to utter such in the midst of uncertainty, in the middle of difficulty, in the center of suffering, but it also recognizes there is something greater at work in us and beyond us.

Gratitude calls us to a naked spirituality, to live out in the open, and therein is the perceived holy danger of it all.

Again, we are confronted with the mystery of vulnerability. Adam and Eve walked naked in the garden where all was peaceful, where all that grew out of the ground, or upon it, coexisted in harmony. They lived out in the open. Everything touched them. All was felt and explored and named. They hid from nothing until they believed a lie and plucked and ate. Then they stole sky-bred leaves to cover their life-giving parts and hid from God.

Maybe it all comes down to this—we've been hiding from God and each other ever since. It is not God who hides from us. The unwillingness to feel and know and name the world, to allow everything—thorn and thistle as well as salt and sea—to sting us, to refuse to live out in the open, is where ingratitude thrives, our fertility dies, and our breasts harden. Ever since that day, we've been taking what is not ours to take. We swallow stones rather than starlight.

To practice gratitude is to practice wakefulness, to discover what was lost, to stop our thievery. Gratitude is a yearning, a longing, a recognition, a response, an expansion. Inside it is a voice, calling us to come out of hiding.

Love,

S

great

really

Hello my dear

RECEIVED

Dear Alice!

Thank you very much

Simplicity

Dear Daughters,

One day, I drove past a piano lying on its side at the end of the driveway and couldn't help but write a poem about it that was later published in *Journal of New Jersey Poets*.

A PIANO

lies on its unbroken spine
hammer heart still within its wire ribs.
It gasps for the breath of fingers
in its wooden and ivory soundlessness.

A corpse, I think, bones waiting their crush,
dignity splintered forever, mouth open
screaming to no one, to everyone.
I drive past. I do not stop.
It cries to my silences.

A clashing symphony of ending.
Keys no longer horizontal, tipped upside down,
like rungs of Jacob's ladder, fallen,
waiting for someone's climb toward God.

It stood once, in a room, against
a wall, in the house at the beginning
of the lane. Before it was a tree,
tusks of animals, ebony from Asia,
before it was grafted together—

all the dark songs of the tree,
the cacophony of distant places,
the ancient hums of roots,
and the invisible music of polishing hands
hunger for freedom, for an ear
to hear, for those small child's chipped
shell fingernails to break the ache
of its muteness

giving speech to angels,
an aria to the wind.
Lyrics to the tongue
of a deaf soul.

I hope this poem brings attention to the songs that are lost,
never sung, abandoned and silenced when we think they are
not worth listening to, when the world rejects our voice, the
speech of our hands, our being.

We are given a name we need to inhabit and sing out.
Everything about us, how we choose to live, speaks us into
existence. So consider the power of simplifying your life.
Declutter your physical environment so that things don't
get in the way, so that you don't end up tossing away the

very thing you need to fully live—be it a piano, a guitar, a desk, an easel, a workshop, a telescope—whatever tools or instruments are necessary for you to grow into yourself. Resist the temptation to be buried alive. When you enter the place you call home, ask yourself if it invites you to sigh with relief or tense with anxiety because what you face comforts or overwhelms you.

Every day I drive by a stone building that looks like it was a one-room schoolhouse a century ago. Outside there is a car stuffed with what looks like clothing. By the front door are piles of things the old woman who lives there moves around daily. At night, you can see mountains of furniture through the windows, objects almost touching the tall-peaked ceiling. This woman spends her hours moving things from one place to another. I see the world in her life, the ways we spend our days moving stuff around.

Ask yourself, If I had a twenty-minute warning to evacuate my home, what would I take? What's most important to you? Work to live your life around a central, worthy-of-life, single-minded focus. When I've asked writing students this question, they always listed the same things: photographs, journals, anything that has a story, memory, or meaning attached to it.

I've had to start fresh several times in my life. It's always difficult to leave things I loved behind, but sometimes we must lose the things we are so attached to, to live for what is most important. Sometimes we need to shed all that clings to us and weighs us down.

Create an environment where you can thrive, where enough "light" gets in, where you do not fill your space with stuff that demands so much of your time and energy that you lose your clear sense of purpose. Order is beauty.

Develop a vision board—a visual depiction of your passion and purpose, the goals you want to achieve, and places you want to go, for starters. We think in images, not words. Arrange pictures on a bulletin board or poster board and glance at them daily. Where you focus is, there you will go.

I ask that you take this exercise seriously, work at it, revise it as you go along. Think—where do you want to be in one year, in five years? What degree do you want to earn? Where do you want to live? What job do you want?

You can intersperse the images with words. Look through magazines or print out pictures that excite you. When you have arranged your images, ask yourself what's missing, what am I not addressing? Fitness? Health? Relationships? Look at what holds your center focus and arrange the images around the one that speaks directly to your passion.

Without intention and an eye on tomorrow, we will walk blindly through our life, or we will not walk at all. Our hearts and minds, when in agreement, will be a force to be reckoned with. Most of us have divorced mind from heart, putting provision in front of passion and purpose. All three must work together. If all one focuses upon is provision, greed easily seeps in. Consider this, the word provision speaks to being *for* one's *vision*.

So much of what we spend our energy and finances on is to protect our vulnerability, our fear of being unloved or unlovable, unacceptable and unworthy. Materialism can be a substitute for what one does not possess—a sense of ultimate purpose, an attempt to prove one's importance or superiority or worth, a substitute for an underdeveloped spiritual life. We are not here to serve stuff.

It's intriguing why storage units are one of the fastest-growing businesses in our country. We are laying "waste our powers" with all of our "getting and spending." I imagine that woman in the stone house finds comfort in her things that may one day fall and crush her.

I confess that I find comfort surrounded by books, blank journals, writing utensils, paper—but these speak of who I am, what my passion is, and my life's work. I find pleasure in being surrounded by photographs of loved ones and places I've been, faces I see on my wall, and my every glance toward them is a prayer.

Be intentional. When we are aware of the sacred in us and our thing to do, clarity comes as does the desire to live a spacious, simple life where courage can grow and originality surface. Then we become our most authentic selves.

Work toward living a transparent life, free from debilitating debt, planet-killing consumerism, and detritus. Declutter and prioritize your surroundings. Outside your dwelling, do whatever is necessary, even if it means picking up your neighbor's garbage. Drive less and work from home whenever possible.

Ultimately, ask yourself whether you want to be an ornamental garden others admire, or an orchard intended to nourish others? We, and the generations that follow us, reap what we grow.

So live naked. Let the world know by one glimpse of your environment what heart beats in you, what longings live in you, what passion and purpose are yours. Order your space so that you can always find what you are living for.

Love,
S

Stone Babies

Dear Daughters,

Many years ago, I read a newspaper article about a woman who carried a stone baby inside her for over fifty years, discovered only after her death. The fetus had died during an abdominal pregnancy and was too large to be reabsorbed by the mother's body, so the unborn ossified.

I can't think of a better metaphor for what remains *unlived* in us, whether dreams, adventures, or desires. They die.

Resentments, betrayals, shame, unresolved anger, secrets, unforgiveness and fear, doubt, unbelief in oneself, perhaps more than all else, calcify our unborn life. We fear our innate aliveness, for it is vast and wild, yet contained in this house of flesh and spirit. Adventure calls out to map the far reaches of what exists within us. Everything is there, all the world. Here we are clay, we are malleable. Here we know the hands and the breath of who will never be contained.

I've traveled to many countries, to places not on any tourist itinerary, and I will write about such journeys in another letter. But the key singular lesson of my travels to faraway and dangerous places is simply this. I had to pass through a dark shroud of fear that clung to me like a second skin. I was afraid of the unknown, of danger perceived and real, as I crossed continents and entered strange lands, cultures, and tribes. I saw and touched and felt that the same hands on me were upon every person.

Fear sentences us to life imprisonment. We are life-givers, fierce in our love, creative, sustainers, birthers, yet our lack of belief in ourselves shackles us. Afraid of what is beautiful and mighty within us, fearful of our sheer strength and resilience, we allow memories, voices, culture, others, and power structures to be our jailers. Break free. Fearlessly rebuild your lives when your bones collapse on top of one another due to an abusive relationship, a significant failure, a deep sorrow. Celebrate and live fully.

Confess the secrets that harden you. They are like stones that cry out that no one hears except you. Silence the forbidding shame. Speak them out loud.

Confession requires a tongue dipped in courage. I've seen women deliver stone babies and free up room inside themselves once they acknowledged the moral injuries that screamed out between their bones, whatever that injury was, whether it be infidelity, sexual abuse, or other life-stealing trauma. Since the beginning of time, women have been prisoners of silence.

We carry other stones, too, that go undetected yet weigh us down. Someone I considered a close friend for most of my life betrayed me. Twenty-five years of absence later, he called as an act of "recovery." After the call ended, it was as if I could hear the thud of a stone falling out of me that I didn't even know I was humping around. It had become part of me, hidden away.

Friends tell me the same story, how they didn't know

the weight of unresolved conflicted relationships until there was a reconciliation. I've wondered throughout the years if the stones we carry aren't the same we hurl at others. When we reach adulthood, do we shore up an entire nursery full of them?

I encourage you, daughters, to find genesis within yourselves. Live free. Be prolific. Trust yourselves to be up to the task of living an unstuck life.

Love,

S

Winter

Dear Daughters,

Winter, like suffering, is a season of darkness that some-times comes overnight. Everything is cold—we can't hold on to anything. All that falls into us, falls out of us. We don't dare speak the name of anything. We are skinless—everything hurts that touches us.

Suffering appears as a cold contradiction to life itself, but it doesn't last forever. It comes as a season, like winter, when we go inward and sometimes need to isolate from others. We come face-to-face with our aloneness. We begin to measure the distance of separation from ourselves and others.

Winter teaches us what no other season can, how we are never truly alone. It tutors us on survival and the necessity for community. That is the paradox of us. We are alone, we are never alone, and we can't do it alone. When we are hurting, the presence or lack of community, that intimate circle of fellow human beings who willingly are a soft place for us to fall, is a matter of what feels like life and death.

There will be times in your lives when sorrow is so

profound, pieces of it have to be broken off and given to those who will care for you. Let them. Let them be present even in your isolation.

Most of us have never learned how to be there for another, especially during grief. Only one thing matters— show up, be present, and revere silence. Do not say, "I know how you're feeling." Let their tears stain your hands and face. Step into the awful, gut-wrenching agony as frightening as it may be and do not move away.

Built into suffering is the possibility of transformation and redemption. Redemption asks that we consent to be broken and pieced back together again, never quite the same person again, but somehow one of greater depth, wisdom, compassion, wonder, and, yes, vision.

In grief, consent to step away from the ever-moving, tilted world. Light a solitary fire against dark skies, press open the spines of blank books, and lift a pen to write out the impossible, illegible vocabulary of sorrow. Reach deep inside and pull out the bloodied words that embody the hurt and make visible what churns inside. Once on the page, suffering has a life of its own outside of us and the act begins to make room for hope within us.

Even in the deepest trouble, there is a longing for aliveness, a hidden holiness, a mysterious unfolding, a revelation. We must learn to revere the mystery of not knowing.

I met seventy-year-old Raimundo Garcia Franco a few years back while in Cardenas, Cuba, and his story illustrates this mysterious unfolding. He spent his teenage years as an underground guerrilla fighter as part of the Revolutionary Resistance Movement during Baptista's corrupt regime when secret police carried out wide-scale violence, torture, and public executions, ultimately killing thousands of Cubans. Franco sabotaged the transportation system, burned buses with Molotov cocktails, littered roads with barbed wire and nails, and set fire to local sugar cane fields. Eventually, when Castro came to power, Franco became a leader in the Radicalization of the Revolutionary Movement. He confiscated land from landowners and became a militia leader of the farmer patrols in his town.

Although he was heavily armed, he said he never killed anyone. But, in time, he realized that he was part of the same violence that he had fought against earlier as the government eliminated private businesses and families were lined up and executed.

Franco had an existential crisis and quit the militia after five years. He said he didn't deserve to be alive, which he often said during our interview. His crisis of conscience continued until he found faith, entered seminary, and became a pastor.

By 1964, the Revolutionary government had turned against the church and forbade religion. Cuba was declared a socialist state. If people attended church, they were considered ignorant, risked being fired from their jobs, were discriminated against, and ridiculed in public. Franco defied the local authorities by increasing the size of the sanctuary, and a short time later, they sent him to a labor camp.

Franco managed to smuggle a small New Testament into the camp and a blank book where he wrote day after day about his experiences, hiding it in his underwear. He lived and worked alongside other dissidents and enemies of the state in the sugar cane fields under unbearable conditions. Priests, pastors, Catholic high school students, criminals, drug addicts, artists, and homosexuals were all the revolution's forbidden people.

The prisoners were allowed one day off a week. On Sundays, Franco and the other priests and ministers held clandestine bible studies, gathering two or three at a time under a tree to discuss Scriptures and share communion secretly.

Two years later, the labor camps closed under the pressure of the Cuban people. Franco returned home, determined to do what he could to preserve the church and improve relations between church and state to prevent such tragedies from ever happening again. But the national Baptist organization he was ordained under wanted no part of such reconciliation efforts. Franco had to choose between serving the church or pursuing his passion.

He chose his passion for working toward peace and reconciliation with the government. He founded the Christian Center for Dialogue and Reflection, an inclusive inter-Christian and inter-religious center where leaders and laypeople come from around the world to discuss theology, ethics, and social justice. The center also has an organic farm to help feed the people of his country. The Center for Reflection and Dialogue stands out like a pearl in a sea of ruin when you are walking down the hot and broken streets of Cardenas. Its walls gleam, the grounds are beautifully sculpted, and the buildings sparkle in the white Cuban sun.

Cuba has suffered behind the rusted Iron Curtain. Homes are crumbling and the average citizen exists on the equivalent of twenty US dollars a month. In Franco's home, as we sat at the kitchen table, he turned the head of a wide-eyed owl figure toward me and said, "The government is listening."

Franco was not willing to sacrifice what was born out

of his tribulation. Out of the hidden holiness within him came the revelation, passion, and vision for his future.

In tragedy, there is a possibility of transformation. Think about justice reforms, how Meagan's Law began, how legislated new gun laws followed the Sandy Hook Elementary School shootings, how the Civil Rights Movement started. They were all born out of suffering.

When trouble comes, and it will, remember it's for a season, like winter itself, that comes after seasons of rebirth, heat, and falling. Temperatures drop, doors shut, snow comes, brightening the earth as if from a cold sun. What falls from heaven replenishes the underground aquifers where faith pools and will flow again in time.

Saint John of the Cross said that everything that happens is grace. This is a hard truth, a difficult lesson, one we never learn without the privilege of time. But nature tells the story again and again of wounding and healing. Just consider myrrh, a coveted oil used to anoint ancient kings and for its medicinal properties. The oil is harvested by repeatedly injuring the myrrh tree to secrete a resin. Like the myrrh tree, we are repeatedly wounded. Will grace flow from us?

In winter, in trouble and grief, stare at the bare forest and what it reveals in its nakedness. Consider the crooked limbs, rough bark, places where life is gone, branches that wait to plummet to earth. Like the forest, we are wild, abundant, and dappled with light. Trees teach us to come out of hiding and stretch toward the heavens in all our vulnerability.

Love,

S

Already

FRANCE

great

really

RECEIVED

ville my dear

Dear Alice!

Thank you very much ...

PARIS

Travel

Dear Daughters,

Photographs of men, women, and children from around the globe hang on my walls. Someone asked me once why all the pictures were of faces, out of the thousands of photos I have taken on my travels. "Faces tell a story," I said. They are maps of ancestry and history, privilege and poverty, power and oppression. Their eyes reflect the world they live in and the world that lives in them. Every day, I remember the Kenyan mother standing outside her mud home, the aging Cuban woman propped against a wall in mid-collapse, one of India's sons begging roadside, exiled old men in Siberia, a veiled woman shepherd in Morocco's Atlas Mountains, and Palestinian children behind an impossible wall.

I've traveled to many countries not as a tourist but as a witness, wandering where few would want or dare to go. The world broke into me as I broke into it.

Mark Twain wrote, "Travel is fatal to prejudice, bigotry, and narrow-mindedness, and many of our people need it sorely on these accounts. Broad, wholesome, charitable views of men and things cannot be acquired by vegetating in one little corner of the earth all one's lifetime."[11]

Such fatalities occur if we allow prejudice, bigotry, and narrow-mindedness to die. If we volunteer to enter the discomfort, as well as the intrigue, of foreign places and peoples. Some people travel to escape themselves, but we are like turtles—we carry our homes on our backs, taking with us our troubles and attitudes. But it is into these homes we carry around, into our shell-like beings, that we make room for *the other*. Is there anything more spiritual than the hospitality of strangers, received or given?

Witnesses listen, record, and honor stories of people and places. They leave no trace, unlike tourists who immerse themselves in the beauty and history of a destination, yet may leave a trace—of judgment, xenophobia, or ignorance.

When traveling, hear the humanity that is never lost in translation and understand that we all share the same mother tongue. Lose yourselves for a time—forget itineraries, just wander, observe, be still, engage in conversation, eavesdrop, journal, photograph, be fully aware of your surroundings, especially as women in foreign countries.

Once, the military personnel warned me not to walk alone on the beach along the Persian Gulf in Saudi Arabia as men would attempt to buy me.

"I just want to see how much they'll offer," I said.

The response? "You don't understand. They will just kidnap you."

Walk the streets of villages and cities. Taste food from local vendors—soak your senses to gain some intimate understanding of where you are. What natives cook, what they eat, will tell you of the fields and oceans beyond the cities and their labors.

I've slogged through the slums of Kenya, India, and Pakistan and seen the poor bent in reverence to touch the feet of a Pakistani prince. I've watched a middle-aged couple dance in their small wooden abode on Lake Baikal's shores near Mongolia's border with Russia. I've experienced the chaos of communism's collapse on an overnight train from St. Petersburg to Moscow when the first-class cabins were robbed while its passengers slept to the rhythmic clanking of locomotion. The conductor was under suspicion for the heist since the cabins locked from the inside. A professor from the University of Alabama, who had traveled to Russia over thirty times, said that under communist rule, he could leave his wallet on his berth and the cabin door open, and no one would dare steal it.

Organized crime flourished in the vacuum left by the fall of communism as the country struggled to define its new freedom. An older Jewish couple, leaning on canes as they walked the streets of Moscow, shared how they feared anti-Semitism that was resurfacing among the people. I conversed with those protesting on the streets who wanted communism back.

During a three-day train ride from Moscow to Irkutsk in Siberia, chugging through the Ural Mountains, I joined a half-dozen Americans in the dining car one evening. We sang Western tunes, ballads, and pop music. After each song, the women working the dining car, sitting across from us, sang a Russian song to us. We exchanged a dozen tunes, and we laughed. One never needs a translator for such dialogues.

On that same train, a couple from Ukraine invited a few of us to share some vodka as we heard the story of how their lives were being reborn. They were starting a new capital business. Then, during a midnight stop somewhere in Siberia, the conductor and an older woman passenger waltzed under the stars.

Having traveled to dozens of countries, I've witnessed how although we do not share the same culture, language, or history, we do share the same longings for passion and meaning. We are siblings of a lost paradise. Our gardens may be parched or lush, forsaken or inhabited, flat or mountainous, but we are dependent on the same Earth we call home.

We are not such a complicated human geography. It's as if our roots grow through Earth's crust to the other side of the world, like an underground tree of life, connecting us with tribes and clans we will never know. So travel, trading fear for compassion. Be open, kind, and generous with all you meet. If we go soul first, we will see how light bends through each place and person, granting us a glimpse of the larger, the deeper, the eternal.

Journey to as many places as possible and bear witness. Keep a journal of your observations and the conversations you hear or engage in along the way. Bring curiosity as well as deep respect wherever you go.

There is much more to write, but I will restrain, realizing I'm lost in past dreams and rambling on. The people and places I've encountered are forever tattooed on my conscience. I remember them. That is why their photographs hang on my walls.

StoryCorps is an organization that records and preserves stories, founded by David Isay, who said that sometimes when you are "really" listening to stories, "you can almost see sparks flying out of someone's mouth. There's just this kind of magnificence and grace to the story."[12]

May you see in all your travels, whether to a neighborhood not your own or somewhere far, far away, sparks of sacred fire flying out of mouths and hands and eyes. And may they land upon you as magnificence and grace.

Love,

S

Creativity

Dear Daughters,

Throughout my letters, I've written to you about what it means to be women of sacred fire. I've encouraged you to explore the mysteries of solitude, loneliness, beauty, aging, and wonder that rumble through our dark, scarlet blood and thunder in our hands and feet. Do not ignore them. They are like lightning, exposing in flashes of light both the *Presence* within us and our unseeable souls. What we see in that sudden luminosity is what's imprinted upon us, like a fossil of something ancient.

I've pressed you to question everything, and that includes your faith or lack of faith, however you identify. Name what is beneath and inside your desire for passion and purpose and meaning. Identifying the name or names is essential if you are to live in your skin, give what is yours to give, and discover the source of your energy, what I've named the *Presence,* and sometimes God, in these letters. In your questioning, start by observing everything around you. The big things. Consider the order and rhythm of our days, time itself, gravity, seasons, tides. What is beneath them? What are these telling you?

During my most faith-starved times, what convinced me above all else of a benevolent *Presence* was my overwhelming urge to create. From then on, I was convinced, and still am, that I was created to create. When lost in creativity, it's as if I've reentered a paradise where life thrives, where there is innocence, where eternity exists. There I begin to know my true self and the *Presence* that is everywhere yet hidden, that requires this kind of stillness and waiting, this kind of showing up. To create, at least for me, is to gaze upward and know I am gazed upon. It's a gaze inward, knowing I am seen from the inside out.

Humans share great pleasure in fashioning something with their hands, minds, and bodies. We bear children, paint pictures, build homes and skyscrapers, color, cook, write poems, compose music, solve equations. This energy, this drive, can be used to construct or de-construct, to build or destroy. It's a matter of humility.

Novelist Kurt Vonnegut wrote in *A Man Without a Country*, "The arts are not a way to make a living. They are a very human way of making life more bearable. Practicing an art, no matter how well or badly, is a way to make your soul grow, for heaven's sake. Sing in the shower. Dance to the radio. Tell stories. Write a poem to a friend, even a lousy poem. Do it as well as you possibly can. You will get an enormous reward. You will have created something!"[13]

Fan the flames of the sacred fire that burns in you and in us all. Creativity offers us a glimpse of eternity and leads us to live in a constant secret communion with wonder. We are, each one of us, but one flame of a great fire. Do not let it burn out. Do not let anyone or anything or any failure extinguish it, only let it flame brighter, burning away what doesn't belong, including the dousing thoughts that you are not good enough or that you have no talents or gifts. Find your thing to do by the light of this fire. We are artists all.

My daughters, your longings hold secrets. Do not abandon or neglect them.

Love,
S

Already

great

really

RECEIVED

Hello, my dear

Dear Allie!

Thank you very much ... your father!

$$\mathcal{P}\text{rovision}$$

Dear Daughters,

Divide the word provision into two parts—*pro* means for, and *vision* means to foresee. Live into the vision you have of your life in everything you do. Don't get derailed, no matter what.

Unless you are highly privileged and inherit wealth, which can be more of a curse than a blessing, learn the dignity of work. All honest work performed honestly will build a good life and teach you the satisfaction of a job well done. Jobs train us to show up even when we don't want to, perform duties we don't enjoy, and submit to the dreaded time clock. Throughout our working lives, we will work with those we may not like or respect, but everyone has something to teach us.

Work is a discipline, a humbling, and a mirror. It shows us our motivations, stick-to-it-ness, engagement, or our disengagement (laziness). It reveals if we are persons of integrity, if we are honorable, helpful, committed, and congenial. Who are we when the boss, or no one else, is looking? One of the highest compliments we can receive is that we are hard workers. To say this more simply, who we are at work is who we are anywhere.

Everyone should do manual labor of some kind, especially when they are younger, to experience the physical toll so many pay all their lives. Such jobs teach us compassion and appreciation for those who work with their hands, their bodies, who suffer for it—the ironworker, painter, farmer, truck driver, migrant worker, coal miner, road crew—the list is long of the uncelebrated.

Above all, whatever work is yours to do at any moment, do more than you are asked or required to do. Do everything as if your life depended upon it. Love your co-workers and love your foes. Let none of them take you captive with their criticisms or power plays. Instead, let every "job" make you more determined, driven, to attend to the call on your life.

Refuse to use work as an excuse not to pursue your passion and purpose. Actors wait tables, writers work in retail, and musicians bartend to support their art. Everything we do and experience is fodder for creative work. Earn your Ph.D. in humanity by opening up to see, touch, engage, and learn to be present with others. Whatever our hands find to do has meaning and purpose if we give it meaning and purpose.

Your *calling* will require everything you have to give. It will demand strength and perseverance that comes only with the doing—this is the meaning of work.

I labored in the housekeeping department of a local nursing home as my first full-time job the summer I turned sixteen. I remember punching a time clock by seven in the morning, the windowless closet-like locker room where the housekeeping crew stored personal items and smoked cigarettes during fifteen-minute breaks, and the pervasive scent of Pine Sol that soaked into our uniforms and skin. I remember the squeaky pail we pushed from room to room as we squeezed gray water from a stringy mop and the air itself, a mixture of urine, poop, and other body fluids. We ordered and sanitized a patient's world, making their compromised lives a little better. I remember short and long conversations I had with the old men and women who called this home and how they looked at me with longing for what I now understand was for what was lost, gone, irretrievable.

I learned my job from Helen, a woman in her sixties whose husband had black lung from working the coal mines all his life. Coal dust filled his lungs and he could barely breathe, she told me. I saw his struggle on her. She breathed differently when she spoke of him. Helen was a humble woman, childless, who worked until her spine curved under the weight of her labor. Her fingers were red-raw from chemicals, yet she was a crocheting whiz and crocheted me a black and white bikini that I learned the hard way wasn't meant for swimming but sunbathing only. She laughed when I told her how the first wave at the Jersey shore soaked it, then dropped it.

Helen taught me the dignity of labor that summer, beyond my parents, who were industrious, creative, and hard workers, who knew lack and took nothing for granted, having grown up during the Depression. My father, born in 1925, knew hunger and told stories of how he and his single mother had to break furniture to burn for heat and had moved ten times the first ten years of his life. Once, they had to walk miles for a head of lettuce to eat. I am forever grateful for my parents' strong work ethic, self-sacrifice, and determination.

Yet, Helen showed me how outside my immediate family, strangers could become family when working side by side for a common goal. Working among the old, dying, disabled, and abandoned at the nursing home and facing my mortality every day at such a young age made me bond to this kind, humble woman on the edge of old age herself.

I held many jobs throughout my life—pumping gas, waitressing, being a mother's helper, cleaning guest apartments with my youngest strapped on my back, managing a small retail shop, bookkeeping, among others—before I began to make a meager living at what I loved most.

The jobs we end up despising still do a work in us. They motivate us to find a way to live into our passion while teaching us how crucial integrity is in everything we do. Work teaches us we must put in the time.

You may need, as I still do, to wake up hours before everyone else and carve out time to do what you love, to grow your life. I encourage you to sign up for workshops, search for a mentor, partner with someone who will lift you when you fall. Slay the demon of self-doubt.

Vincent Van Gogh sold one painting in his lifetime, yet he knew that he had to live his passion. So here are some of his quotes you might want to tack up on your vision board:

> "Your profession is not what brings home your weekly paycheck, your profession is what you're put here on earth to do, with such passion and such intensity that it becomes spiritual in calling."

"One must never let the fire go out in one's soul but keep it burning."

When I was going through unbearable times, my father said, "Get lost in your work." He finally understood writing was my life's work. Writing was the only place I've ever been truly found, a place that kept me from losing my life to the sorrow and strife of the day, tethered me to the living, and helped me to remember my name.

I am adding a very long poem to this letter that I wrote a long time ago to honor those who have labored before us, upon whose shoulders we stand or fall.

Love,

S

P.S. My grandfather was an uneducated man who knew what it was to work in the fields. This poem celebrates him and the power of work.

Fields

My grandfather told me when he was six-years old
his ma gathered him, his five brothers and five sisters,
one a deaf mute, to abandon home, father, the city
of Syracuse, to travel the countryside, to gather
as he had been, the fruit of the fields.

He remembers squinting his small eyes against the light
and how his tiny hands blistered first,
long before forming dandelion callouses on his palms.
Insects crawled up his arm as if stalks or stems,
looking for a home in his summer homelessness.

Sun burned his olive skin, left its map.
His fingers splintered and gashed with labor.
Creamy blood of beans filled the reservoirs
of them until the skin of the bean
was more familiar than his own.

When it rained, the field buried his toes,
bare, like his parents did two babies
he never knew, born dead.
His feet sank into the cooled earth
like miniature plows.

"My family was so poor. We had to survive.
We worked from six every morning til
eleven every evening, every day."
He earned salvation by hand,
as did his ma, brothers, and sisters.

At night, sleep came on prickly sun-dried hay bales—
the smell of hay seeped deep into his thread-worn
clothes even though his ma tore open flour sacks,
sewed them together for sheets.

Like bread, she kneaded him into place,
pleading with the Virgin for dreams to rise
in him as his brothers breathed into his ears,
a circular wind, blowing beyond the barn
where they were herded like sheep,
like lambs he refused to count.

Morning, he woke, eyelids swollen,
draped like a shroud, like dew over the world.
The only salt left unspent in toil drained
into fissures between muscles
that burned already, before rising.

Songs of childhood fled his body
but not his hands, yanking beans to nursery
rhymes thought forgotten, shuffling seeds
into his forever-hungry mouth alongside his sister,
whose hands yet had no voice.

He wondered if when she crushed seeded fruit
between her jaws, did she feel the crunch of its flesh,
hear it as tremors in her body?
Did she hear its song on each tastebud?
Might her tongue blossom under its sweetness?

He watched her, pausing only for a moment,
his eyes hurting from the brilliant sky,
hoping no one noticed how he stopped to study
the swarm of bodies that were his family of poverty,
brothers and sisters, mothers and fathers,
he would never know.

"My brother grew up to be a priest,"
he said. He found God among the roots of things,
in the ways plants grow, in their dying.
He culled evidence of Eden among the harvest,
in the poor, in his mother's bent back.

His ma worked side by side among them,
her face furrowed yet not so deep.
The field of her fertile belly soft from birth.
Her wrists narrow, too narrow to block the sun
from burning away the first layer of her brood's skin.

Her body gave no shade as she moved row to row
clocking shadows. She'd stop to wipe the shimmer
of sweat from her children's faces even as her own bled
the same; rain-like, rolling down her cheeks in single file
as if the water sought the river that ran to the ocean.

Her lips, cracked white, as if floured.
At their corners, tiny rips edged up, tearing her words.
She pretended he knew, even as a young boy,
that she could protect them from the ways of earth,
the ways wind and fire curve their spine,
break their backs.

Her womb so heavy-laden and ripe,
began its fall from her like an over-ripe peach.
Poverty was a thief of their childhood, she told him,
making sons men before they were boys
and daughters women before they were girls.

She'd say in her Italian accent, "See that bean
severed from its vine, its mother so young,
only to die for someone else to live?
That's the way of the world."
She'd shake her head. "Torn, separated, sold."

My grandfather says he misses her,
wishes he could care for her as she did all of them,
but she passed long ago.
He's an old man now, and his skin
is damp with heat and memory.

Back then, sometimes he'd tuck a few bean pods
into his pockets, sideways, so that they wouldn't fall
through the holes, for later hunger that always came.
Then jade pulp would wedge between his teeth,
the rest filling his fist-size stomach.

Acquainted, he said, with the architecture
of each bean held in his palm, the snap it made
when he split open the pod. Squatting close to ground
he reaped the mysteries of earth in private,
tonguing the raw seeds in his mouth.

He measured the width and quadrangle of him,
cast on the ground as the sun grew and withered him.
Felt the nubby hairs of beans and their crooked seams
and sipped the inside water, so thirsty midday.
Sometimes he'd save the seeds, bury them in his pockets,
but they'd shrivel after a few days in the parched
darkness, spent on the cotton field of his pants.

Still, he'd eat them, wondering if they would
awaken and grow inside of him.
If someone snapped him open, would they find
seeds collected in the pockets between his ribs?

He knew his ribs—traced them with his fingers
at night thinking they were bean-like,
both sides growing toward each other,
his stomach the basket, his heart the sun.

But he felt no warmth or light in the center of him,
only a thumping like feet prodding toward the fields
every morning. When he dreamed, he felt his feet too,
heading some other place, but his ankles shackled.

He told me about the terrain of those fields,
how they dipped and rose like his own body,
like the spaces between his knuckles,
and how his bones are probably half-beans now.
He hears them snap sometimes when he bends
or falls or twists the wrong way.

I look at the land of his hands, the color of freshly
turned soil, river-smooth, navy veins irrigating
his old man flesh. He reaps raspberries now,
carefully resting each berry into an empty coffee can,
his gentle hands tugging, embracing, then sliding
the berry away from its home.

A choreography his hands can't forget.
Lines deep in his palms, unplanted.
After he dies (he says that will be soon),
things will grow out of them.

He knows this, having buried old brothers
and his silent sister whose voice is a part
of the underground streams. He hears her, he says.
He slips a raspberry into his hand.
It looks like a heart, broken and healed,
scarred into clusters, and he breaks
the gathering apart at their seams.

Juice stains like sorrow.
"I miss my ma. I wish she were alive,"
he says again. "I would take care of her now."

He holds his fist half-open, raises it to his tongue,
and lays it there for a moment before closing his mouth
around its sweet blood trickling
over and down into muscles
fraying from bone, into the field within him
that waits for the harvest.

Already

great

really

Dear Alice!

Thank you very much

RECEIVED

Invest

Dear Daughters,

Let me add a few more words about provision since this may be the most difficult aspect of living a passionate, purposeful life. Rarely does provision come easily when we are in pursuit of our calling, our thing to do above all others. In many ways, it serves us better when it doesn't. Difficulty, despair, and discouragement are not enemies of the life you are called to live, but refiners of it.

I don't believe in magic or in magical thinking. I don't believe wishing something makes it happen or speaking a word out "into the universe" is anything more than speaking out loud one's desires or fears. However, I consider myself a mystical thinker. I believe in mystery, in what cannot be fully known even as the sense of deep-down knowing ripens in us. I believe "the universe" has a personal name, and I call upon that name. This life requires a good deal of exploration and excavation of mystery so that we walk around dazzled by wonder, all the while taking up the tools of commitment, disciplined work, focus, vision, and fortitude, drawing ever closer to the sacred fire that burns within every one of us.

Learn to value what is yours to do, what is yours to give, while encouraging others to do the same. Do not sell your soul to the highest bidder or to the bottom line, to a lesser love, or for the love of the other. A verse in the Hebrew Bible says, "Invest in truth and never sell it—in wisdom and instruction and understanding."[14]

I pray these letters are an investment in truth, wisdom, instruction, and understanding. By now you have figured out that Rainer Maria Rilke is one of my favorite writers and poets who wrote that "in order to be, it is not enough to be born;" we must "ripen until we are real." And, "The sense people have of impermanence and perishing comes mostly from their own not-having-been-ness."[15] Too many women lament their own not-having-been-ness too late in life.

The sacred fire aflame inside of you will singe and sear and char and leave scorch marks. But it will also light the way as you feed the flame, reflect its light, warm the earth, and create a contagion in others to stoke the fire within them. So live from the inside out, not from the outside in. Go with the adventure, trust the *Presence*, make the passage, live conscious of the mystery you are and of the Mystery of Mysteries.

Where will provision come from? How will it come? From a million different places and ways. Only invest in truth.

Love,

S

Time

Dear Daughters,

Cheat death. I wrote in my journal during the height of the pandemic in January of 2021 after losing a friend to COVID:

> "I rise in winter darkness to see if I can catch a glimpse of the first sunlight, almost as if I could defeat or defy the night within myself and keep death at bay. I stare the sky in the face, awake to beauty I cannot yet see. I rub constellations into myself as I sit down to write about what I cannot know. Sipping coffee is like bathing my body in chocolate, sweetening and stirring and stilling time."

Cheat death by not sleeping your life away or wasting time on what doesn't matter. Rise early. There's too much to do that only you can do.

I cringe when I hear people say they are killing time. For me, that is to murder oneself. Time is the one gift most are desperate to buy at the end of their lives, so cultivate a sense of urgency, for time is as thin as light and as ungraspable. When we are young, we think we have all the time in the world to do this thing or that. We think time is endless, but it isn't. I can't tell you how many times I hear people in their fifties and sixties and beyond say, "Life is so short," and there is always an urgency in their voice. Time has wings, and it can never be captured.

A tyrannical mathematician, time calculates hours and days into seasons and years on an invisible abacus. It's a hard-core reality, a mystery. Somehow, what is past is still with us even as the future hovers, as if we are always living in a state of in-betweenness. Yet do not be afraid to mourn what is behind you, lament what you must, freeing it from defining your future.

Some people say I've lived an amazing life. If that's true at all, it's because I know time owns me. I don't own it. I know that somehow time lives inside eternity—and as I write that, I can't explain what that means other than there is a timelessness to our lives, so it's crucial to live ever conscious of the benevolent *Presence*. Our lives are in motion even after we are gone. So, love well.

Don't let others dictate how you should spend your days. Time is currency, and be careful where you spend it. Live with a sense of urgency, rise before dawn, call forth your passions, and draw constellations in the dark hours. Bathe your body in chocolate. Know what is unknowable. Still time.

Love,

S

Regrets

Dear Daughters,

I have regrets. When people say they have none, I think they are lying, mostly to themselves. We are imperfect beings living an imperfect life. We hurt others knowingly or unknowingly, and when we do, innocent of intent or not, we are hurting ourselves as well. Is that not worth lamenting on both fronts? Such people say that everything that's happened, their choices for good or for bad, has shaped who they are today. Some of us might argue that is precisely why they should have some regrets! It's the worst kind of pride, making a person unapproachable, unreachable, unreal.

If only I had, if only I hadn't, frames what we grieve when we look back, and many of us don't look back soon enough. Psychologists say that sixty is the age of review when we stare backward and count the costs or the losses, likely because when we turn around, we realize there is more behind us than in front of us. Perhaps the most common regret is that we lacked the courage to do the thing we were called to do. What pains me the most when I speak to older women—and the reason for including this letter— is when I hear them say they never risked, feared failure too much, or allowed others to hold them back or down. Most distressing is when women say they suffer an "unused" life and resign themselves to an unfinished life.

In the British newspaper, *The Guardian*, a palliative care nurse reported the top regrets of the dying that she, Bronnie Ware, witnessed. One, "I wish I had the courage to live a life true to myself, not the life others expected of me," was according to Ware, the most common regret of all. At the end of life, vision is most clear and people see how many dreams were abandoned or not honored due to choices made or not made. She added, "Health brings a freedom very few realize until they no longer have it."

Two, particularly among men, "I wish I hadn't worked so hard." Ware noted that this came from every male patient she cared for. In her words, "They missed their children's youth and their partner's companionship." They grieved "spending so much of their lives on the treadmill of a work existence."

Three, many wished they had spoken up, expressed their emotions. In other words, they'd kept the peace despite the storm that raged in them. Again, in Ware's words, "As a result, they settled for a mediocre existence and never became who they were truly capable of becoming. Many developed illnesses relating to the bitterness and resentment they carried as a result."

Lastly, people regret not paying enough attention to their friends and wished they had let themselves be happier as they dreaded change, were too attached to safety and comfort, and to old ways of being.[16]

I've written to you of what exiles us from ourselves and others, but other lifestyle choices take their toll—smoking, drinking, gambling, overeating, and spending too much.

Each "health" choice is a path we choose, often ignoring or denying where it ultimately leads.

Surveys and studies also conclude that women regret failed love relationships.[17] Listed among women's biggest regrets are not trying hard enough at school, choosing the wrong career path, spending a night with someone they shouldn't have, not being spontaneous enough, not being a good enough friend, not being a better daughter, not traveling before starting a family, not having children, not being a better mom, having an affair, getting married and settling down, and focusing too much on their career.

You will inevitably have regrets, but I'm hoping these letters will count for something, shed some light in the darkness, offer a hand in the middle of the night, and encourage you to live for higher things and live more fearlessly. So many opportunities don't come around twice, and sometimes you just have to follow your gut.

I pray, daughters, that you will have the courage to toil on and not give up on yourself or others. Don't practice defeat. Learn self-compassion. Most of us will need it when we look back on our lives and see missed adventures, unexplored landscapes, loved ones we left behind, and silencing and neglecting the call upon our lives.

Grief over what is lost or never found, the path not taken, is not the enemy. The enemy is when we refuse to acknowledge the regrets so that we might change course, confess, make amends, and honor the companions who join us along the way.

Love,

S

Earth

Dear Daughters,

Listen to the wild. Listen to snow falling, rain on your windowsill, shifting ice. Everything is alive. Insects buzz, birds chirp, leaves chatter, rivers hum. Each sound utters a prayer to live. So, listen with every cell of your being to the earth, away from the clamor of human company and constructs.

Being still, paying attention, listening to the natural world, heals us body and soul. Studies show that we are wide awake, focused, and relaxed when we are attentive to nature. There's a good reason for that. We are made of the same song. Hear in everything, the beginning of everything, the sacred strain chanted over everything. All that exists plays a note in this great chorus—wind and rain, trees and sky, sea and shore; every crawling, flying, walking, and pouncing creature. Lions roar, monkeys hoot, coyotes howl, catfish growl.

They sing to live and make the world aware of their right to exist. But listen. If you listen carefully enough, you will also hear the most awful sound of all—the sound of what is being lost and the raging wildfire that we humans are. It's as if the Tree of Life and the Tree of Death are rubbing together, combusting into flame, destroying and silencing that song. I hear it in the tornado ripping through our lands, tearing lives to shreds. I feel it in the soaring temperatures that bake our fields and forests. I witness it in the parched wilderness, crackling with drought. I lament it in the elegy of tens of thousands of species becoming extinct every year.

Listen, and you will hear the terror of their absences. This earth is as close to heaven as we will ever come to in our lives. And we are its hell.

If we want to live a fertile life, we must stop murdering our mother. We must protect the fertility of the plant and animal kingdoms. This listening isn't about attending to the interior life, or interrogating solitude and wonder. This is a recognition, a reckoning, a repentance of the ways we contribute daily to the destruction of the planet—each one of us. Everything we do or don't do impacts the near and far, the present and future. Wail against silent springs. Work toward the salvation of all creation, for our provision comes from the earth alone.

Daughters, protect the world's fertility, and you will protect your own.

Love,

S

Revolutionaries

Dear Daughters,

We are like trees. Whatever one you are—mahogany or magnolia, walnut or willow, acacia or aspen—offer refuge from the heat, shelter for the forsaken, and fuel for fire.

Whatever privilege is yours, use it for the sake of righting the wrongs and working toward justice for every tribe on Earth. You will accomplish nothing without humility, kindness, and compassion, which will grow out of your struggles, difficulties, and hardships. I know of no other way to become agents of transformation or lovers of humanity. Without these virtues, we will do more damage than good. Anger will not achieve justice, nor will violence end violence.

Compassion means *to suffer together*. Think of the heroes who entered the fray, walked with others, and worked for radical change without violence: Mother Theresa, Rosa Parks, Pauli Murray, Erin Brockovich—the list is endless. Some women most will never hear of, like twenty-five-year-old Kabita Bhandari, known as the cloud-walker, who scales icy cliff sides and leaps over rushing rivers to bring contraceptives to the most remote villages in the Himalayan mountains. Or Farzana Akbari, who stood up against virginity tests in Afghanistan to protect women and girls from these invasive, discriminatory, and unscientific, never mind humiliating exams.[18]

Zen Buddhist Monk Thich Nhat Hanh taught that our life must be our message and that we suffer less when we have compassion because compassion compels us to act, to enter into the suffering of another. The Good Samaritan had mercy on his cultural and religious enemy, left to die on the side of the road after being beaten and robbed. The Samaritan was a secret agent of change, acting "behind the scenes" on the human stage, not for recognition, but simply because it was right.

That's how revolutions begin—inside of us, with our willingness to see, challenge, step up, and risk. First, we must grow deep and steadfast in the garden entrusted to us so that we can withstand the storms that will come. Our taproot, that large, central, and dominant root from which all other roots grow out from, must be anchored in love, faith, and hope. We need not look for what must be done. It is in front of us, looking us in the eye and asking if we have the courage to act.

We will be equipped to work toward justice when we have lived justly and stood up to the opponents who stand in our way—the greatest ones being fear, apathy, complacency, and comfort. That's how our taproot grows strong and deep, drawing from underground rivers where our ancestors swim, and how fire shoots up into our branches. For how can we walk with another in their suffering when we have fled our own? Suffering has the power to cleanse us if we let it, if we surrender to it for the season it insists on staying. If we resist, we wither, our souls shrivel, our clay hearts harden.

Faithfully journal as I've encouraged you in earlier letters—this is one way we let suffering in to wash over us, scrub our pores, rinse our tears. I have wondered if *Suffering* is the name of the angel who stands guard at the entrance to the *Garden of Presence*, and one can only enter in through her, who holds a fiery sword in her hand. Maybe this is why few enter paradise in this life.

Paper serves as an echo chamber. Maybe it's because we, like trees and paper itself, are life distilled. Hear the words on it, across it, within it. By the tenth sentence, or more or less, what we think we should write fades away and honesty emerges since we have a natural aversion to lies, self-delusion, and phoniness. So write toward what is most dangerous within you until the skies unfasten and the darkness evaporates. Write until you are emptied and can listen no more. Write as an act of creation, revolution, redemption, and salvation. To quote author, poet, and social activist Alice Walker, "Writing saved me from the sin and inconvenience of violence."

I do not understand the power or the mystery of writing, or the voice that rises inside of it like underground lightning. I can see my breath in words as if they are exhaled from the winter inside of me, all white, like a dream uttered into the world, revealing what I cannot comprehend. As I wrote in my first letter, words on a page are scorch marks. In writing, we decipher the colors of sacred flame that alight the angel's fiery sword—the violets, blues, yellows, oranges—pigments of heaven and earth.

Leave this life with nothing more to give. Provide

refuge, shelter, and fuel to others. Let every branch of your being be luminous.

Love,
S

Generosity

Dear Daughters,

Daughters of sacred fire, after the wildfires come, live resurrection. Resurrection lives in you, in us, evident with every wound that heals. It's the mystery of light spoken into our dark blood.

Work out your salvation with fear and trembling, the good book says, which is not to say let fear imprison you. I believe it means never give up, do what is given to you to do, work until it works its way out of you and into the world no matter what may come. Be fully engaged in the magnificent struggle and refuse to miss your life or sacrifice the greater for the lesser, the difficult for the easy. Follow the narrow way, not the path of least resistance. Then you will tremble with wonder and awe and grace. Working out your salvation requires a whole-hearted focus. Trembling requires yourself, body and soul, to live into the sacred.

A life consecrated by passion, which gives meaning to everything you do and organizes your days around a central desire and mission, will also be your greatest vulnerability. Rejection will come. But grit, dignity, integrity will be the fruit of your perseverance if you remain steadfast.

Herein is the most startling and perplexing mystery of all. You will only fully possess your life and grow into it if you choose to give it away. And you can only give it away if you truly possess it. The more you give what's been given you, the deeper and more profound your living will be.

Living is terminal for those who do not fully possess or lose their lives for the sake of the love—love is the end game of the passionate, purposeful life that will outlive us. So be faithful to your calling that is both individual and specific, as well as collective and universal.

Live artful, transparent lives so that when others gaze upon you, they will see the source of your aliveness and long to bathe in its light and warmth. If we love humanity with all the intensity with which we are loved, we have the possibility of sharing with others the deepest communion available to us—a human holy communion that awakens the longings in us for what is beyond the boundaries of time and Earth, what never dies.

We can only know the fullness of *Presence* together. Each one of us offers a glimpse if the flame burns high enough. You can only give what is yours to give. So tilt the world toward this communion of healing, mercy, and compassion, toward the resurrection within us all.

Passion and purpose will not lead to provision without perseverance. Provision is not magically given, but if you set your life in motion toward the greatest purposes, it will come.

You will have trouble. Press on through the wildfires of rejection, loneliness, loss, self-doubt. All of these have the potential to purify and refine you. A worthy life is never without its labor and charred places. Honor your being and all that lives in you.

Daughters, stoke the embers of your highest life-giving passion for the sake of the world. Hold on to the wild in you. Joy is cultivated in those who love and commune with the creative sacred spirit of resurrection.

Love,

S

I hope you enjoyed reading these letters to our daughters as much as I enjoyed writing them for you. Please visit your favorite online retail store to leave a review.

Your feedback is very important to me!

About the Author

Reverend Sherry Blackman is the pastor of The Presbyterian Church of the Mountain in Delaware Water Gap, Pennsylvania, home to the oldest, continuously running Hiker Hostel on the Appalachian Trail. She is an award-wining, internationally published journalist, poet, and author of *Call to Witness*, a true story of one woman's battle with a disability, discrimination, and a pharmaceutical powerhouse, and *Tales from the Trail: Stories from the Oldest Hiker Hostel on the Appalachian Trail*. Her forthcoming book, *Rev-It-Up: Tales of a Truck Stop Chaplain*, due out in 2022, chronicles her adventures as a Truck Stop Chaplain, a ministry she's served since 2006. Rev. Blackman is also a chaplain with the Pennsylvania State Police.

Visit the author's website: sherryblackman.com

Reach out to the author at: revblackman@gmail.com

Acknowledgments

I would like to acknowledge all the women in my life who I could never name in their entirety, for the ways they have loved and nurtured me, beginning with my family—my mother, Shirley; my sister, Sandy; daughters Erin and Lindsay; granddaughters Harley and Destiny; friends who are always with me: Nancy, Toni, Cynthia, Denise…too many to name.

I would like to honor all women who didn't take no for an answer, who I will never know personally but who made a way in the many wildernesses women face every day.

Thank you, Debra L Hartmann, from The Pro Book Editor for your expertise, friendship, and for catching me when I was in mid-fall.

Endnotes

1 Helen Thomson, "A Third Of Women Are More Afraid Of Loneliness Than A Cancer Diagnosis." (Dec 18, 2017)

2 Stefanie Groner, "The Fear of Being Alone Is Real—Here's How to Face It." (Jan 27, 2021)

3 Rainer Maria Rilke, *Rilke's Book of Hours: Love Poems to God* (Riverhead Books, New York, Nov 2005)

4 C. S. Lewis, *The Four Loves* (Geoffrey Bles, January 1, 1960)

5 Timothy D. Wilson et al. "Just think: The challenges of the disengaged mind." *Science* Vol 345, Issue 6192, pgs 75-77 (4 Jul 2014)

6 Marianne Williamson, *Return to Love: Reflections on the Principles of A Course in Miracles* (Harper Collins, 1992) Retrieved from: https://marianne.com/a-return-to-love/

7 Charles Martin, *Long Way Home* (Thomas Nelson, 2016)

8 Carl Sagan, *Cosmos* (Ballantine Books) Retrieved from: https://ia800401.us.archive.org/32/items/Cosmos-CarlSagan/cosmos-sagan.pdf

9 Fyodor Dostoevsky, *The Brothers Karamazov* (1880)

10 William Wordsworth, "The World Is Too Much With Us" Retrieved from: https://www.poetryfoundation.org/poems/45564/the-world-is-too-much-with-us

11 Mark Twain, *The Innocents Abroad*, (SeaWolf Press; Illustrated edition July 30, 2018)

12 Norah O'Donnell, "Bridging America's political divide with conversations, 'One Small Step' at a time." (Jan 9, 2022)

13 Kurt Vonnegut, *A Man Without a Country* (Nabu Press; Primary Source ed. edition, October 6, 2013)

14 https://biblehub.com/bsb/proverbs/23.htm

15 Rainer Maria Rilke, *Rilke's Book of Hours: Love Poems to God* (Riverhead Books, New York, Nov 2005)

16 Susie Steiner, "Death and dying: Top five regrets of the dying." (Courtesy of Guardian News & Media Ltd., Feb 2012)

17 https://www.yourtango.com/201173966/most-women-regret-failed-relationships-more-than-anything-else

18 https://www.unfpa.org/news/league-extraordinary-women-real-life-super-heroes